EARLY INVENTIONS

Julie Haydon

Contents

Rigby

Inventions

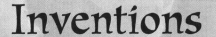

What would life be like without tools, clocks, wheels, and writing?

All these things are **inventions**.

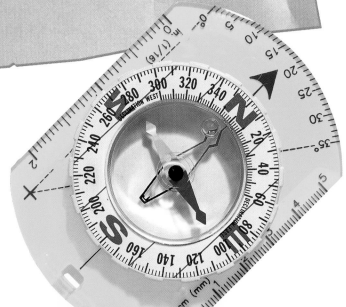

2

Inventions are new things
that change how
we work and play.
Inventions make life easier.

3

Stone Tools

Long ago, people lived in caves. They hunted animals for food and skins. They cut wood for their fires and dug up roots to eat.

stone tools

They invented stone tools
to make these jobs easier.

The Plow

When people began to live in villages, they kept animals and grew crops.

New tools were needed to work the land. The **plow** was invented.

The first plow was a stick.
Farmers used the stick
to break up soil.

7

Over time, a handle and a wooden **blade** were added to the stick.

Later, animals were used to pull the heavy plow.

The Wheel

When the first wheel was invented,
it looked like a round table.
A potter spun the wheel
and shaped clay on it.

The first cartwheels were made of wooden planks.
The wheels were very heavy.

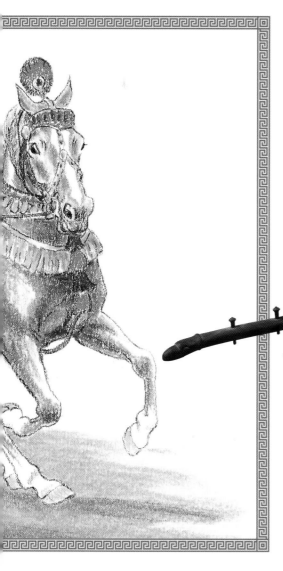

spokes

People wanted
to make wheels lighter.
They invented **spokes**.

13

Writing

People invented writing to pass on messages and to keep **records**.

They used pictures for words.
They used a sharp reed
to draw the pictures onto clay.

15

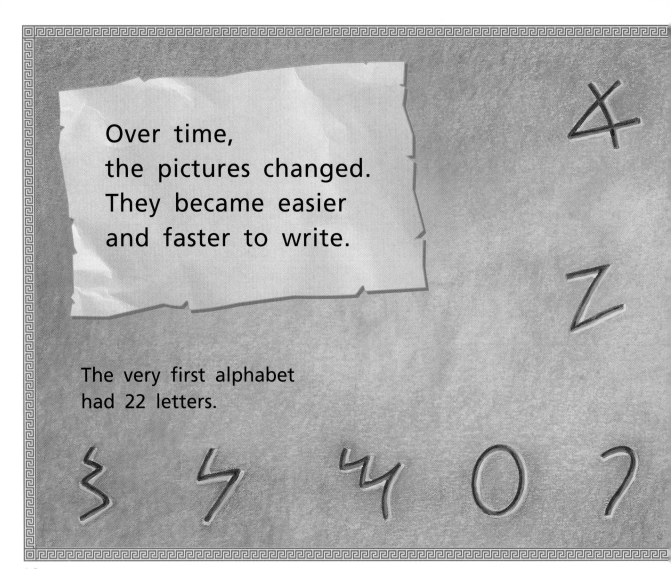

Over time,
the pictures changed.
They became easier
and faster to write.

The very first alphabet
had 22 letters.

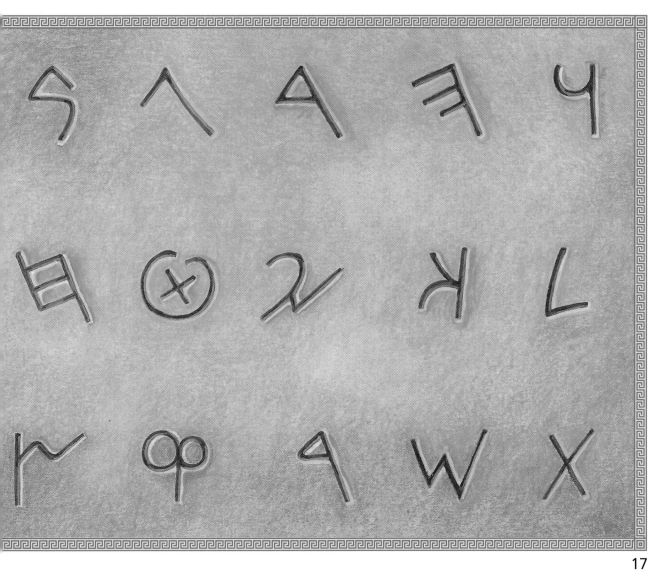

17

Telling the Time

The clock was invented to tell the time.

The first clock was a simple stick. The sun shone on the stick and made a shadow. People looked at how long the shadow was.

Later, the sundial was invented.
The sundial is a clock, too.
Sunlight shone on the sundial
and made a shadow.
The shadow
told people
the time.

The Compass

The compass was invented to show direction.

This compass was invented long ago. It was made of **magnetic rock**.

The compass looked like a spoon.

The spoon would spin on the board. When it stopped, its handle always pointed south.

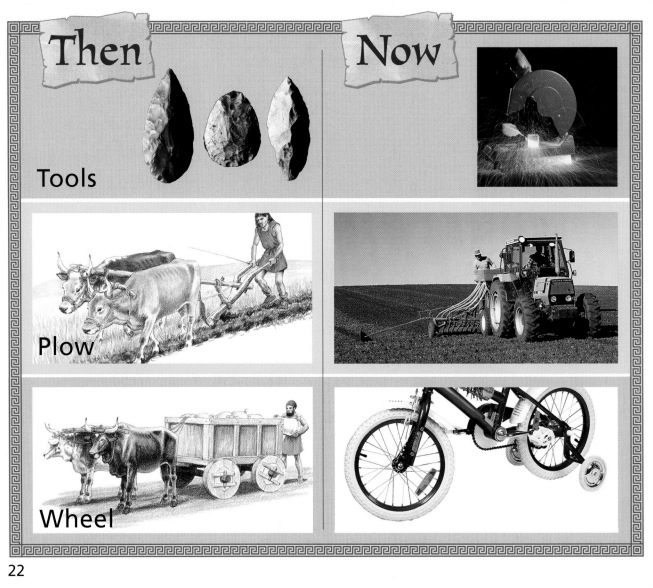

Then

Now

Tools

Plow

Wheel

Then | **Now**

Writing

Telling the Time

Compass

23

Glossary

blade a sharp part of a tool used for cutting

inventions new things that change the way we work or play

magnetic rock a rock that is a magnet

plow a tool used in farming to turn over soil

records information that is written down

spokes thin bars that run from the center of a wheel to its rim

Index